DAY  SURFER

LOGIN ORGANIZER

Johnson & Hunter, Inc. Peachtree City, Georgia 30269

© 2012 Johnson & Hunter, Inc.

Printed in the United States of America

ISBN-13: 978-1-933598-57-4

Disclaimer: Recording or providing private confidential information always carries a risk of loss or damage from that information. You should be sure about all risks involved, and you always assume full personal responsibility for this risk. You are strongly recommended to store your information securely. It is your responsibility to update your information frequently. When possible, it is recommended that you abbreviate a password if it is used on more than one website.

We do not accept or assume any responsibility or liability for use by others, loss, theft, accidents or injuries as a result of your decision to purchase or obtain this organizer and record confidential information of yourself or others.

Company

URL

User Name

Password

Notes

Company

URL

User Name

Password

Notes

Company

URL

User Name

Password

Notes

Company

URL

User Name

Password

Notes

Company

URL

User Name

Password

Notes

A

Company

URL

User Name

Password

Notes

Company

URL

User Name

Password

Notes

Company

URL

User Name

Password

Notes

Company

URL

User Name

Password

Notes

Company

URL

User Name

Password

Notes

A

Company

URL

User Name

Password

Notes

Company

URL

User Name

Password

Notes

Company

URL

User Name

Password

Notes

Company

URL

User Name

Password

Notes

Company

URL

User Name

Password

Notes

A

Company

URL

User Name

Password

Notes

Company

URL

User Name

Password

Notes

Company

URL

User Name

Password

Notes

Company

URL

User Name

Password

Notes

Company

URL

User Name

Password

Notes

Company
URL
User Name
Password
Notes

Company
URL
User Name
Password
Notes

Company
URL
User Name
Password
Notes

Company
URL
User Name
Password
Notes

Company
URL
User Name
Password
Notes

B

Company

URL

User Name

Password

Notes

Company

URL

User Name

Password

Notes

Company

URL

User Name

Password

Notes

Company

URL

User Name

Password

Notes

Company

URL

User Name

Password

Notes

B

Company

URL

User Name

Password

Notes

Company

URL

User Name

Password

Notes

Company

URL

User Name

Password

Notes

Company

URL

User Name

Password

Notes

Company

URL

User Name

Password

Notes

B

Company
_____
URL
_____
User Name
_____
Password
_____
Notes

Company
_____
URL
_____
User Name
_____
Password
_____
Notes

Company
_____
URL
_____
User Name
_____
Password
_____
Notes

Company
_____
URL
_____
User Name
_____
Password
_____
Notes

Company
_____
URL
_____
User Name
_____
Password
_____
Notes

_____

Company

URL

User Name

Password

Notes

C

Company

URL

User Name

Password

Notes

Company

URL

User Name

Password

Notes

Company

URL

User Name

Password

Notes

Company

URL

User Name

Password

Notes

C

Company

URL

User Name

Password

Notes

Company

URL

User Name

Password

Notes

Company

URL

User Name

Password

Notes

Company

URL

User Name

Password

Notes

Company

URL

User Name

Password

Notes

C

Company

URL

User Name

Password

Notes

Company

URL

User Name

Password

Notes

Company

URL

User Name

Password

Notes

Company

URL

User Name

Password

Notes

Company

URL

User Name

Password

Notes

C

Company

URL

User Name

Password

Notes

Company

URL

User Name

Password

Notes

Company

URL

User Name

Password

Notes

Company

URL

User Name

Password

Notes

Company

URL

User Name

Password

Notes

D

Company
URL
User Name
Password
Notes

Company
URL
User Name
Password
Notes

Company
URL
User Name
Password
Notes

Company
URL
User Name
Password
Notes

Company
URL
User Name
Password
Notes

D

Company

URL

User Name

Password

Notes

Company

URL

User Name

Password

Notes

Company

URL

User Name

Password

Notes

Company

URL

User Name

Password

Notes

Company

URL

User Name

Password

Notes

Company

URL

User Name

Password

Notes

D

Company

URL

User Name

Password

Notes

Company

URL

User Name

Password

Notes

Company

URL

User Name

Password

Notes

Company

URL

User Name

Password

Notes

D

Company

URL

User Name

Password

Notes

Company

URL

User Name

Password

Notes

Company

URL

User Name

Password

Notes

Company

URL

User Name

Password

Notes

Company

URL

User Name

Password

Notes

Company

URL

User Name

Password

Notes

Company

URL

User Name

Password

Notes

Company

URL

User Name

Password

Notes

Company

URL

User Name

Password

Notes

Company

URL

User Name

Password

Notes

Company
URL
User Name
Password
Notes

E

Company
URL
User Name
Password
Notes

Company
URL
User Name
Password
Notes

Company
URL
User Name
Password
Notes

Company
URL
User Name
Password
Notes

Company

URL

User Name

Password

Notes

E

Company

URL

User Name

Password

Notes

Company

URL

User Name

Password

Notes

Company

URL

User Name

Password

Notes

Company

URL

User Name

Password

Notes

Company

URL

User Name

Password

Notes

E

Company

URL

User Name

Password

Notes

Company

URL

User Name

Password

Notes

Company

URL

User Name

Password

Notes

Company

URL

User Name

Password

Notes

Company

URL

User Name

Password

Notes

F

Company

URL

User Name

Password

Notes

Company

URL

User Name

Password

Notes

Company

URL

User Name

Password

Notes

Company

URL

User Name

Password

Notes

Company

URL

User Name

Password

Notes

F

Company

URL

User Name

Password

Notes

Company

URL

User Name

Password

Notes

Company

URL

User Name

Password

Notes

Company

URL

User Name

Password

Notes

Company

URL

User Name

Password

Notes

Company

F

URL

User Name

Password

Notes

Company

URL

User Name

Password

Notes

Company

URL

User Name

Password

Notes

Company

URL

User Name

Password

Notes

Company

URL

User Name

Password

Notes

F

Company

URL

User Name

Password

Notes

Company

URL

User Name

Password

Notes

Company

URL

User Name

Password

Notes

Company

URL

User Name

Password

Notes

Company

URL

User Name

Password

Notes

Company

URL

G

User Name

Password

Notes

Company

URL

User Name

Password

Notes

Company

URL

User Name

Password

Notes

Company

URL

User Name

Password

Notes

Company

URL

User Name

Password

Notes

Company

URL

User Name

Password

Notes

Company

URL

User Name

Password

Notes

Company

URL

User Name

Password

Notes

Company

URL

User Name

Password

Notes

Company

URL

User Name

Password

Notes

Company

URL

User Name

Password

Notes

Company

URL

User Name

Password

Notes

Company

URL

User Name

Password

Notes

Company

URL

User Name

Password

Notes

Company

URL

User Name

Password

Notes

Company

G **URL**

User Name

Password

Notes

Company

URL

User Name

Password

Notes

Company

URL

User Name

Password

Notes

Company

URL

User Name

Password

Notes

Company

URL

User Name

Password

Notes

Company

URL

User Name

Password

H

Notes

Company

URL

User Name

Password

Notes

Company

URL

User Name

Password

Notes

Company

URL

User Name

Password

Notes

Company

- -

URL

- -

User Name

- -

Password

- -

Notes

Company

- -

URL

- -

User Name

- -

H **Password**

- -

Notes

Company

- -

URL

- -

User Name

- -

Password

- -

Notes

Company

- -

URL

- -

User Name

- -

Password

- -

Notes

Company

- -

URL

- -

User Name

- -

Password

- -

Notes

- -

Company

URL

User Name

Password

Notes

Company

URL

User Name

Password

Notes

H

Company

URL

User Name

Password

Notes

Company

URL

User Name

Password

Notes

Company

URL

User Name

Password

Notes

Company

URL

User Name

Password

Notes

Company

URL

User Name

H **Password**

Notes

Company

URL

User Name

Password

Notes

Company

URL

User Name

Password

Notes

Company

URL

User Name

Password

Notes

Company

URL

User Name

Password

Notes

Company

URL

User Name

Password

Notes

I

Company

URL

User Name

Password

Notes

Company

URL

User Name

Password

Notes

Company

URL

User Name

Password

Notes

Company

URL

User Name

Password

Notes

Company

URL

User Name

Password

Notes

Company

URL

User Name

Password

Notes

Company

URL

User Name

Password

Notes

Company

URL

User Name

Password

Notes

Company

URL

User Name

Password

Notes

Company

URL

User Name

Password

Notes

I

Company

URL

User Name

Password

Notes

Company

URL

User Name

Password

Notes

Company

URL

User Name

Password

Notes

Company

URL

User Name

Password

Notes

Company

URL

User Name

Password

I Notes

Company

URL

User Name

Password

Notes

Company

URL

User Name

Password

Notes

Company

URL

User Name

Password

Notes

Company

URL

User Name

Password

Notes

Company

URL

User Name

Password

Notes

J

Company

URL

User Name

Password

Notes

Company

URL

User Name

Password

Notes

Company

URL

User Name

Password

Notes

Company

URL

User Name

Password

Notes

Company

URL

User Name

Password

Notes

Company

URL

User Name

Password

Notes

Company

URL

User Name

Password

Notes

Company

URL

User Name

Password

Notes

Company

URL

User Name

Password

Notes

Company

URL

User Name

Password

Notes

J

Company

URL

User Name

Password

Notes

Company

URL

User Name

Password

Notes

Company

URL

User Name

Password

Notes

Company

URL

User Name

Password

Notes

Company

URL

User Name

Password

Notes

J

Company

URL

User Name

Password

Notes

Company

URL

User Name

Password

Notes

Company

URL

User Name

Password

Notes

Company

URL

User Name

Password

Notes

Company

URL

User Name

Password

Notes

Company

K

URL

User Name

Password

Notes

Company

URL

User Name

Password

Notes

Company

URL

User Name

Password

Notes

Company

URL

User Name

Password

Notes

Company

URL

User Name

Password

Notes

K

Company

URL

User Name

Password

Notes

Company

URL

User Name

Password

Notes

Company

URL

User Name

Password

Notes

Company

URL

User Name

Password

Notes

Company

URL

User Name

Password

Notes

Company

URL

User Name

Password

Notes

K

Company

URL

User Name

Password

Notes

Company

URL

User Name

Password

Notes

Company

URL

User Name

Password

Notes

Company

URL

User Name

Password

Notes

K

Company

URL

User Name

Password

Notes

Company

URL

User Name

Password

Notes

Company

URL

User Name

Password

Notes

Company

URL

User Name

Password

Notes

Company

URL

User Name

Password

Notes

Company

URL

L

User Name

Password

Notes

Company

URL

User Name

Password

Notes

Company

URL

User Name

Password

Notes

Company

URL

User Name

Password

Notes

Company

URL

User Name

Password

Notes

L

Company

URL

User Name

Password

Notes

Company

URL

User Name

Password

Notes

Company

URL

User Name

Password

Notes

Company

URL

User Name

Password

Notes

Company

URL

User Name

Password

Notes

Company

URL

L

User Name

Password

Notes

Company

URL

User Name

Password

Notes

Company

URL

User Name

Password

Notes

Company

URL

User Name

Password

Notes

Company

URL

User Name

Password

Notes

Company

URL

User Name

Password

Notes

Company

URL

User Name

Password

Notes

Company

URL

User Name

Password

Notes

Company

URL

User Name

Password

Notes

Company

URL

User Name

Password

Notes

Company

URL

User Name

Password

M

Notes

Company

URL

User Name

Password

Notes

Company

URL

User Name

Password

Notes

Company

URL

User Name

Password

Notes

Company

URL

User Name

Password

Notes

M

Company

URL

User Name

Password

Notes

Company

URL

User Name

Password

Notes

Company

URL

User Name

Password

Notes

Company

URL

User Name

Password

Notes

Company

URL

User Name

Password

Notes

Company

URL

User Name

Password

M

Notes

Company

URL

User Name

Password

Notes

Company

URL

User Name

Password

Notes

Company

URL

User Name

Password

Notes

Company

URL

User Name

Password

Notes

Company

URL

User Name

M Password

Notes

Company

URL

User Name

Password

Notes

Company

URL

User Name

Password

Notes

Company

URL

User Name

Password

Notes

Company

URL

User Name

Password

Notes

Company

URL

User Name

Password

Notes

N

Company

URL

User Name

Password

Notes

Company

URL

User Name

Password

Notes

Company

URL

User Name

Password

Notes

Company

URL

User Name

Password

Notes

Company

URL

User Name

Password

N | **Notes**

Company

URL

User Name

Password

Notes

Company

URL

User Name

Password

Notes

Company

URL

User Name

Password

Notes

Company

URL

User Name

Password

Notes

Company

URL

User Name

Password

Notes

N

Company

URL

User Name

Password

Notes

Company

URL

User Name

Password

Notes

Company

URL

User Name

Password

Notes

Company

URL

User Name

Password

Notes

Company

URL

User Name

Password

N Notes

Company

URL

User Name

Password

Notes

Company

URL

User Name

Password

Notes

Company
_____
URL
_____
User Name
_____
Password
_____
Notes

Company
_____
URL
_____
User Name
_____
Password
_____
Notes

Company
_____
URL
_____
User Name
_____
Password
_____
Notes

O

Company
_____
URL
_____
User Name
_____
Password
_____
Notes

Company
_____
URL
_____
User Name
_____
Password
_____
Notes

_____

Company

URL

User Name

Password

Notes

Company

URL

User Name

Password

Notes

Company

URL

User Name

Password

Notes

O

Company

URL

User Name

Password

Notes

Company

URL

User Name

Password

Notes

Company

URL

User Name

Password

Notes

Company

URL

User Name

Password

Notes

Company

URL

User Name

Password

Notes

O

Company

URL

User Name

Password

Notes

Company

URL

User Name

Password

Notes

Company
- -
URL
- -
User Name
- -
Password
- -
Notes

Company
- -
URL
- -
User Name
- -
Password
- -
Notes

Company
- -
URL
- -
User Name
- -
Password
- -
Notes

O

Company
- -
URL
- -
User Name
- -
Password
- -
Notes

Company
- -
URL
- -
User Name
- -
Password
- -
Notes

- -

Company

URL

User Name

Password

Notes

Company

URL

User Name

Password

Notes

Company

URL

User Name

Password

Notes

Company

URL

User Name

Password

Notes

P

Company

URL

User Name

Password

Notes

Company

URL

User Name

Password

Notes

Company

URL

User Name

Password

Notes

Company

URL

User Name

Password

Notes

P **Company**

URL

User Name

Password

Notes

Company

URL

User Name

Password

Notes

Company

URL

User Name

Password

Notes

Company

URL

User Name

Password

Notes

Company

URL

User Name

Password

Notes

Company

URL

User Name

Password

Notes

P

Company

URL

User Name

Password

Notes

Company

URL

User Name

Password

Notes

Company

URL

User Name

Password

Notes

Company

URL

User Name

Password

Notes

P

Company

URL

User Name

Password

Notes

Company

URL

User Name

Password

Notes

Company

URL

User Name

Password

Notes

Company

URL

User Name

Password

Notes

Company

URL

User Name

Password

Notes

Company

URL

Q

User Name

Password

Notes

Company

URL

User Name

Password

Notes

Company

URL

User Name

Password

Notes

Company

URL

User Name

Password

Notes

Company

URL

User Name

Password

Notes

Company

URL

User Name

Password

Notes

Company

URL

User Name

Password

Notes

Q

Company

URL

User Name

Password

Notes

Company

URL

User Name

Password

Notes

Company

URL

User Name

Password

Notes

Company

URL

User Name

Q

Password

Notes

Company

URL

User Name

Password

Notes

Company

URL

User Name

Password

Notes

Company

URL

User Name

Password

Notes

Company

URL

User Name

Password

Notes

Q

Company

URL

User Name

Password

Notes

Company

URL

User Name

Password

Notes

Company

URL

User Name

Password

Notes

Company

URL

User Name

Password

Notes

Company

URL

User Name

Password

Notes

Company

URL

User Name

Password

Notes

R

Company

URL

User Name

Password

Notes

Company

URL

User Name

Password

Notes

Company

URL

User Name

Password

Notes

Company

URL

User Name

Password

Notes

Company

URL

User Name

R | **Password**

Notes

Company

URL

User Name

Password

Notes

Company

URL

User Name

Password

Notes

Company

URL

User Name

Password

Notes

Company

URL

User Name

Password

Notes

Company

URL

User Name

Password

Notes

R

Company

URL

User Name

Password

Notes

Company

URL

User Name

Password

Notes

Company

URL

User Name

Password

Notes

Company

URL

User Name

Password

Notes

Company

URL

User Name

R | **Password**

Notes

Company

URL

User Name

Password

Notes

Company

URL

User Name

Password

Notes

Company

URL

User Name

Password

Notes

Company

URL

User Name

Password

Notes

Company

URL

User Name

Password

Notes

S

Company

URL

User Name

Password

Notes

Company

URL

User Name

Password

Notes

Company

URL

User Name

Password

Notes

Company

URL

User Name

Password

Notes

Company

URL

User Name

Password

S Notes

Company

URL

User Name

Password

Notes

Company

URL

User Name

Password

Notes

Company

URL

User Name

Password

Notes

Company

URL

User Name

Password

Notes

Company

URL

User Name

Password

Notes

S

Company

URL

User Name

Password

Notes

Company
_____

URL
_____

User Name
_____

Password
_____

Notes

Company
_____

URL
_____

User Name
_____

Password
_____

Notes

Company
_____

URL
_____

User Name
_____

Password
_____

Notes

Company
_____

URL
_____

User Name
_____

Password
_____

S Notes

Company
_____

URL
_____

User Name
_____

Password
_____

Notes

_____

Company

URL

User Name

Password

Notes

Company

URL

User Name

Password

Notes

Company

URL

User Name

Password

Notes

Company

URL

User Name

Password

Notes

T

Company

URL

User Name

Password

Notes

Company

URL

User Name

Password

Notes

Company

URL

User Name

Password

Notes

Company

URL

User Name

Password

Notes

Company

URL

User Name

Password

Notes

T

Company

URL

User Name

Password

Notes

Company

URL

User Name

Password

Notes

Company

URL

User Name

Password

Notes

Company

URL

User Name

Password

Notes

Company

URL

User Name

Password

Notes

T

Company

URL

User Name

Password

Notes

Company

URL

User Name

Password

Notes

Company

URL

User Name

Password

Notes

Company

URL

User Name

Password

Notes

Company

URL

User Name

Password

Notes

T

Company

URL

User Name

Password

Notes

Company

URL

User Name

Password

Notes

Company

URL

User Name

Password

Notes

Company

URL

User Name

Password

Notes

Company

URL

User Name

Password

Notes

Company

U

URL

User Name

Password

Notes

Company

URL

User Name

Password

Notes

Company

URL

User Name

Password

Notes

Company

URL

User Name

Password

Notes

Company

URL

User Name

Password

Notes

U

Company

URL

User Name

Password

Notes

Company
_____

URL
_____

User Name
_____

Password
_____

Notes

Company
_____

URL
_____

User Name
_____

Password
_____

Notes

Company
_____

URL
_____

User Name
_____

Password
_____

Notes

Company
_____

URL
_____

User Name
_____

Password
_____

Notes

Company
_____

URL
_____

User Name
_____

Password
_____

Notes

U

_____

Company

URL

User Name

Password

Notes

Company

URL

User Name

Password

Notes

Company

URL

User Name

Password

Notes

Company

URL

User Name

Password

Notes

U

Company

URL

User Name

Password

Notes

Company

URL

User Name

Password

Notes

Company

URL

User Name

Password

Notes

Company

URL

User Name

Password

Notes

Company

URL

User Name

Password

Notes

Company

URL

User Name

V

Password

Notes

Company _____

URL _____

User Name _____

Password _____

Notes _____

Company _____

URL _____

User Name _____

Password _____

Notes _____

Company _____

URL _____

User Name _____

Password _____

Notes _____

Company _____

URL _____

User Name _____

Password _____

Notes _____

Company _____

URL _____

V **User Name** _____

Password _____

Notes _____

_____

Company

URL

User Name

Password

Notes

Company

URL

User Name

Password

Notes

Company

URL

User Name

Password

Notes

Company

URL

User Name

Password

Notes

Company

URL

User Name

Password

Notes

Company

URL

User Name

Password

Notes

Company

URL

User Name

Password

Notes

Company

URL

User Name

Password

Notes

Company

URL

User Name

Password

Notes

Company

V URL

User Name

Password

Notes

Company

URL

User Name

Password

Notes

Company

URL

User Name

Password

Notes

Company

URL

User Name

Password

Notes

Company

URL

User Name

Password

Notes

Company

URL

User Name

Password

Notes

W

Company

URL

User Name

Password

Notes

Company

URL

User Name

Password

Notes

Company

URL

User Name

Password

Notes

Company

URL

User Name

Password

Notes

Company

URL

User Name

W Password

Notes

Company

URL

User Name

Password

Notes

Company

URL

User Name

Password

Notes

Company

URL

User Name

Password

Notes

Company

URL

User Name

Password

Notes

Company

URL

User Name

Password

Notes

Company

URL

User Name

Password

Notes

Company

URL

User Name

Password

Notes

Company

URL

User Name

Password

Notes

Company

URL

User Name

Password

Notes

Company

URL

User Name

W Password

Notes

Company

URL

User Name

Password

Notes

Company

URL

User Name

Password

Notes

Company

URL

User Name

Password

Notes

Company

URL

User Name

Password

Notes

Company

URL

User Name

Password

Notes

XY

Company

URL

User Name

Password

Notes

Company

URL

User Name

Password

Notes

Company

URL

User Name

Password

Notes

Company

URL

User Name

Password

Notes

Company

URL

User Name

Password

XY Notes

Company

URL

User Name

Password

Notes

Company

URL

User Name

Password

Notes

Company

URL

User Name

Password

Notes

Company

URL

User Name

Password

Notes

Company

URL

User Name

Password

Notes

XY

Company

URL

User Name

Password

Notes

Company

URL

User Name

Password

Notes

Company

URL

User Name

Password

Notes

Company

URL

User Name

Password

Notes

Company

URL

User Name

Password

XY Notes

Company

URL

User Name

Password

Notes

Company

URL

User Name

Password

Notes

Company

URL

User Name

Password

Notes

Company

URL

User Name

Password

Notes

Company

URL

User Name

Password

Notes

Z

Company

URL

User Name

Password

Notes

Company

URL

User Name

Password

Notes

Company

URL

User Name

Password

Notes

Company

URL

User Name

Password

Notes

Company

URL

User Name

Password

Notes

Z

Company

URL

User Name

Password

Notes

Company

URL

User Name

Password

Notes

Company

URL

User Name

Password

Notes

Company

URL

User Name

Password

Notes

Company

URL

User Name

Password

Notes

Z

Company

URL

User Name

Password

Notes

Company

URL

User Name

Password

Notes

Company

URL

User Name

Password

Notes

Company

URL

User Name

Password

Notes

Company

URL

User Name

Password

Notes

Z

Company

URL

User Name

Password

Notes

Company

URL

User Name

Password

Notes

Company

URL

User Name

Password

Notes

Company

URL

User Name

Password

Notes

Company

URL

User Name

Password

Notes

Company

URL

User Name

Password

Notes

Company

URL

User Name

Password

Notes

Company

URL

User Name

Password

Notes

Company

URL

User Name

Password

Notes

Company

URL

User Name

Password

Notes

Notes:

Notes:

Other Editions Available

at

www.LoginOrganizer.com

www.ingramcontent.com/pod-product-compliance
Lightning Source LLC
Chambersburg PA
CBHW052148070326
40689CB00050B/2524